SCROLLS, COURTS AND THE SEVEN SPIRITS OF GOD

Written by
Lindi Masters

Illustrated by
Lizzie Masters

Published by

Written by©
Lindi Masters

Illustrated by©
Lizzie Masters

Special thanks to our mentor and friend Ian Clayton, without whom we wouldn't have explored these realms.

Thank you to IGNITE KIDZHUB© for their contributions to the story.

This edition published by
SERAPH CREATIVE in 2018

All rights reserved. No part of this publication may be reproduced, stored in a retrieval system or transmitted, in any form or by any means, electronic, mechanical, photocopying, recording or otherwise, without the prior permission of the copyright holder.

ISBN 978-0-6399842-2-3

CONTENT

The Seven Spirits of God
4-12

Courts
13-16

Scrolls
17-20

KidZhub Artwork
21-24

THE SEVEN SPIRITS OF GOD

The Seven Spirits of God are not The Holy Spirit. They stand before the Throne of God. We call them teachers and governors.

Revelation 1 verse 4

They often teach us in classrooms in Heaven.

They teach us how to do things, not do them for us.

We can be taught by the Seven Spirits of God anytime we want to.

Isaiah 11 verse 1-2

SPIRIT OF THE LORD

Teaches us about the glory of God and government of God.

And everything to do with the dimensions of The Realms of Heaven.

SPIRIT OF UNDERSTANDING

She shows us how and where to go into the Realms of God.

She teaches us to understand revelation and visions.

SPIRIT OF THE FEAR OF THE LORD

Teaches us about the wonders of God.
It doesn't mean we are afraid.
And helps us to mature as Sons.

We go to the Mobile Court by faith. See yourself standing in the Courts.

In the Courts of God we have the Seven Spirits of God to testify for us. The accuser stands on our righthand, accusing us!

We can ask God for forgiveness and to judge our hearts. We know He always forgives us.

Then we can ask God to judge satan the accuser and kick him out of the Court.

We receive our papers and scrolls of forgiveness from those accusations and put them in our heart or eat them.

Zechariah 3 verse 1-7

Isn't it wonderful that as the Children of God, we can go to the Mobile Courts of Heaven and bring judgement to the accuser.

SCROLLS

The Bible talks about scrolls and books. Have you ever seen a scroll before?

In the Courts of Heaven there is a Scroll Room.
The scrolls in this room tell us about everything Yahweh has created and about our lives.

We can go into the Scroll Room and ask the Angels for our life scrolls that were written in the Mountain of Yahweh. Everyone has a scroll that they have agreed to.

We eat the scroll and put it in our hearts and release its sound and frequency.

Thank you Yahweh for the scroll of my life.
Psalm 139 verse 16

KIDZHUB ART WORK

Art work of the Seven Spirits, Courts and Scrolls by the International KidZhub from around the world, including the UK and Australia

Top left: Mobile Courts- Jeiel

Top right: Mobile Court- Hendriette

Bottom left: Throne of Grace- Reuben

Bottom right: Mobile Court- Judah

The spirit of the lord: red
The spirit of wisdom: orange
The spirit of understanding: green
The spirit of Council: yellow
The spirit of knowledge: indigo
The spirit of might: blue
spirit of the fear of the lord: violet

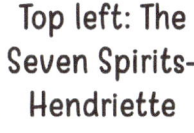

Top left: The Seven Spirits- Hendriette

MOBILE COURT

Top right: Mobile Court- Reuben

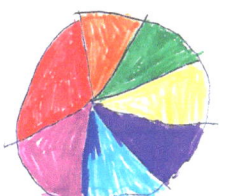

Bottom left: My Scroll- Carla

Bottom right: My Scroll- Ashlyn

Top left and middle: Scrolls- Carla

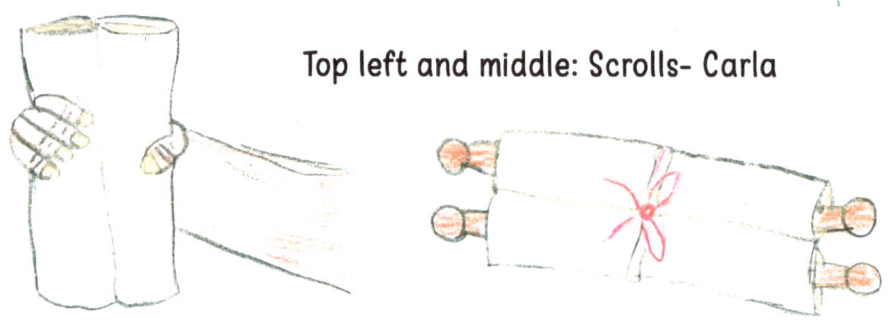

Bottom left: My scroll- Reuben

Top right: My Scroll- Reuel

Bottom right: Scroll- Izak

www.ingramcontent.com/pod-product-compliance
Lightning Source LLC
Chambersburg PA
CBHW041155290426
44108CB00002B/76